PAUL VERLAINE

VERLAINE

FROM A PASTEL BY W. ROTHENSTEIN

PAUL VERLAINE

BY

WILFRID THORLEY

LONDON : CONSTABLE AND COMPANY LTD
BOSTON & NEW YORK: HOUGHTON MIFFLIN COMPANY
1914

PAUL VERLAINE

I

THIRTY-FIVE miles south-west of Brussels
and ten north-east of the French border
stands the town of Mons, known to the
Flemish as Bergen, both names arising
from that ant-hill on which it is set in the
midst of level country. Large dogs tug
eagerly at small milk-carts that rattle
quickly over the square-set stones which
women in sabots are always swilling with
water and scrubbing with stiff, long-
handled brooms. A quaint old clock-
tower perched high over the town rambles
drowsily through a crazy sweet tune to
mark the passage of every quarter, and a
cavalry officer now and then will clatter
out into the untroubled stillness of the
GRAND' PLACE onto which a Gothic Town
Hall looks sleepily and serenely down.

The unwitting tourist, suddenly awaking
here, might be forgiven for assuming that
his good fortune had led him to so picturesque a haunt of ancient peace, where all
the women seem to be intent on having
spotless floors and shining knockers, and
where *Traitez les animaux avec douceur*
appears as a sober admonishment to the
callous from every street corner. But, as
he sat sipping in a neighbouring café, his
ears would be suddenly startled by the
ferocious snort emitted—not by a medieval
dragon—but by the locomotive of the
district street railway which draws up its
coaches beneath the still grey glance of the
sixteenth-century Hôtel de Ville ; and,
following the rails, he would come out on
to a picturesque avenue of trees which
rise from the ancient fortifications of Mons,
and below which, at three miles' distance,
his keen eye might discern tall pyramids of
heaped-up débris, and the chimneys of the
many mills and foundries that stand as a
witness to Belgian prosperity. A hundred
yards further on he would reach a vast
three-sided building from the central pin-
nacle of which there rises the colossal

figure of a flying Mercury. Scores of students might be seen issuing therefrom with a badge set on their long-peaked caps and a sheaf of books tucked under their arms ; for this is the Commercial Institute of the Manufacturers of Hainaut. And here is the site of Verlaine's first penance ; for side by side with this building stands another of lesser height but wider area, whose walls of older and duller brick are slit by the narrowest of windows, and crowned with mock castellations in the manner of a medieval fortress. Along its front groves of trees, their arms crisscrossing, make a clerestory of leaves through which the sunbeams filter down, and heavy vans, guarded fore and aft by blue-garbed officers with white epaulets and a fantasy of looped braid across their breasts, bear prisoners to or from the wide-arched doorway of this the country gaol.

A student glancing through the outer windows of the opposite building, in the intervals of memorizing notes of his " *Produits Chimiques* " or "*Géographie Coloniale*," may see lonely figures moving one within each segment of a circle divided from its centre by high walls that shut them out effectively from all communication with their neighbours in misfortune. He knows that they are enjoying the little spell of free movement that is granted them twice daily in the triangular spaces of this unmoving wheel; he sees them clad in a kind of loose sackcloth, and their faces hidden from the gibes of the mocker by a hood which yields them its grudging peep at the sun through two small holes.

Just forty years ago, among these drab-clothed *détenus*, moved the poor wastrel and wine-bibber Paul Verlaine, French by chance of birth, but a Walloon by derivation of paternal blood. Hither was he brought from the Belgian capital to live out the sentence of two years' imprisonment there passed on him for the attempted assassination of his fellow vagabond Arthur Rimbaud, the sulky, self-centred youth who had settled as a parasite on his slender bounty.

In his bare cell, with an adjustable table that served him for bed each day as the light left him; fed " everlastingly on soup

—of barley, with pea-soup for Sundays," this slant-eyed, snub-nosed, strangely child-like creature paced many weary hours in the presence of one familiar spirit—a brazen crucifix that hung unmoving on the wall.

He might have been glimpsed there, as he was indeed seen in later life, with " a face devoured by dreams, feverish and somnolent ; it had earthly passion, in-tellectual pride, spiritual humility ; the air of one who remembers, not without an effort, who is listening, half distractedly, to something which other people do not hear ; coming back so suddenly, and from so far, with the relief of one who steps out of that obscure shadow, into the noisier forgetfulness of life." Only here he was shut out from life and penned in with his own soul, which brought him quickly to bay, and bade him sue like a penitent child for a reconciliation.

" Shakespeare in English . . . with valu-able notes by Johnson and all the English, German, and other commentators " light-ened the heavy hours, until news of his nullified marriage cast him anew into the deepest slough of despond, and started him on the strange quest for salvation so touchingly recorded in "*Sagesse*."

Mon Dieu m'a dit: Mon fils, il faut m'aimer. Tu vois
Mon flanc percé, mon cœur qui rayonne et qui saigne,
Et mes pieds offensés que Madeleine baigne
De larmes, et mes bras douloureux sous le poids

De tes péchés, et mes mains ! Et tu vois la croix,
Tu vois les clous, le fiel, l'éponge, et tout t'enseigne
A n'aimer, en ce monde ou la chair regne,
Que ma Chair et mon Sang, ma parole et ma voix.

Ne t'ai-je pas aimé jusqu'à la mort moi-même,
O mon frère en mon Père, O mon fils en l'Esprit,
Et n'ai-je pas souffert, comme c'était écrit?

N'ai-je pas sangloté ton angoisse suprême
Et n'ai-je pas sué la sueur de tes nuits,
Lamentable ami qui me cherches où je suis?

From the day of his finding of this " perfect freedom " until the day of his material release, he was, he assures us, perfectly happy ; and if only fortune had sent him a life-sentence we might have been spared the unmerciful disasters that followed his wayward feet, and made the peer of the finest spirits of his time a consort in penury of sluts and felons. His life thereafter was a continual see-saw between whole-hearted wantonness and the rigours of repentance, and he seems to have found each of an equal savour, the lewd and the lovely. How came he to that pass ?

II

At noon on the first day of April, 1844, Nicholas Auguste Verlaine, an Ardennais by birth, and then, in his forty-sixth year, holding responsible rank as captain in a regiment of the French army stationed at Metz, in Lorraine, presented a male child, but two days old, for registration at the Town Hall of the city, a fellow captain of his own brigade and a veteran officer on the retired list accompanying him as witnesses to the deed. All were living in the *Rue Haute Pierre*, whose name, now translated to *Hochsteinstrasse*, reminds the traveller of what, in the hazards of politics and war, has since evolved. Certificate of the birth of Paul Marie Verlaine was thereupon delivered, and the system of revolving in circuits, then as now, imposed on French officers, made this child of a wanderer native of a place with which his forbears were in no way linked, and from which in

12

a year or two he moved with his father's regiment to the sunnier cities of Montpellier and Nimes, in the more classic regions of Provence. A return to Metz and a short stay there was followed by his father's retirement and settlement at Paris, where the young hopeful crowned his studies with the *baccalauréat* in 1862, he being then three years short of his majority. That coming of age was marked by the death of his father, whom Lepelletier, the close friend of Verlaine from his childhood onward and the biographer of his choice, describes as " a tall old man, stern and upright, his thin face tanned and shrivelled, severe in his whole bearing, but in no wise a curmudgeon." The old warrior had started his soldiering at sixteen in the army of the great Napoleon, and had not been so strict a father as he preferred to seem, for he daily visited the boarding-school where Paul was a learner, with inquiries after his health and his diligence ; and with him there always came something toothsome to eke out the frugal fare of the scholar's dining-table.

Left at this critical age without the wholesome incentive of a father's approba-

tion or the restraining fear of his dis-
pleasure, Paul knew only the fond ministra-
tions of a soft-hearted mother who blamed
his boon companions for excesses that were
of his own wilful seeking. " She knew
nothing about literature, and she always
admired her son's works, without understanding them. I am not sure that she ever
read them," writes Lepelletier. " She
adored her Paul, and forgave him everything. In consequence, she had often to
repent of her over-indulgence, and in
silence suffered from her boy's backsliding ; but she did not dare to scold him
when he came home drunk, which was
often enough." A clerkship in an insur-
ance office was soon followed by an appoint-
ment at the Hôtel de Ville, to whose duties
he brought small competence and no zeal.
Married in 1870 to a girl of eighteen,
Verlaine, always keenly susceptible to the
appeal of patriotism, volunteered for the
defence of the capital, though legally
exempt from service ; but soon cold,
fatigue, and his besetting weakness brought
on an attack of bronchitis, and therewith
his retirement from the barricades and sub-

sequent resumption of his official routine. She had been but six months married, and the glowing tribute of *"La Bonne Chanson"* was scarcely completed when the young wife who had inspired it, then ripening towards motherhood, fled to her parents' roof, in disgust and exasperation at his drunken ways and the wranglings to which they incessantly gave rise.

Vous n'avez pas eu toute patience

he wrote reproachfully two years later, and there can be no doubt that the rupture scarred him not the less deeply because brought about by his own wilfulness and ill-temper. The sonnet to which, following a frequent whim, he gave the English title of " Nevermore," and the wonderful " Chanson d'Automne," which are both found in his " *Poèmes Saturniens* " (written somewhere about his twentieth year and before their meeting), have the strange insight of a man who knew himself foredoomed to misfortune in love and in life.

Souvenir, souvenir, que me veux-tu ? L'automne
Faisait voler la grive à travers l'air atone,
Et le soleil dardait un rayon monotone
Sur le bois jaunissant où la bise détone.

PAUL VERLAINE

Nous étions seul à seule et marchions en rêvant,
Elle et moi, les cheveux et la pensée au vent.
Soudain, tournant vers moi son regard émouvant :
" Quel fut ton plus beau jour ? " fit sa voix d'or vivant.

Sa voix douce et sonore, au frais timbre angélique.
Un sourire discret lui donna la réplique,
Et je baisai sa main blanche, dévotement.

—Ah ! les premières fleurs qu'elles sont parfumées !
Et qu'il bruit avec un murmure charmant
Le premier *oui* qui sort de lèvres bien-aimées !

Lecturing in London twenty-five years later, Verlaine refers to this early volume apologetically as a " youthful affair, marked by imitations to right and left ; Hugo, Gautier, Baudelaire, Banville." But the seeds of the later Verlaine are there, though stifled under a burden of exotic terminology and fidelity to marmorean flawlessness of presentment.

III

M. CHARLES DE SIVRY, composer, who was
one of the intimate friends of Verlaine's
opening manhood, lived with his mother
and his stepfather, in a home that was
brightened by the presence of the young
girl Mathilde Mauté de Fleurville, child of
his mother's second marriage. Together
one evening in the house of the notary, her
father, their boisterous chatter and hilarity
were startled into silence by a sudden
knocking on the door, and behind it was
discovered the young stepsister, all abashed
by the temerity of her attempt to enter the
sanctum of the young collaborators and
apologetic for her presumption in desiring
to share the cause of their amusement.
Verlaine was then nearing his twenty-sixth
year, grotesquely ugly, diffident, and
ashamed in the presence of women, among
whom he had no chance of triumphing,
and with whom he had never yet dared to

attempt sentimental relations, though there
is ample evidence that, secretly, he had
long been addicted to vulgar trafficking
with the harpies of desire. " He had,"
says Mr. Arthur Symons, " a face without
a beautiful line, a face all character, full
of somnolence and sudden fire, in which
every irregularity was a kind of aid to the
crayon." At first sight of this romanti-
cally named girl, love entirely mastered
him, and held him happily to its high
discipline with an immediate steadying of
his loose habits that surprised all his
friends. What for him was more astounding, since he well knew the ill attraction
of his ugly features, his devotion appeared
to be returned with an ardour equal to
his own. The knowledge of this was not,
of course, immediately vouchsafed to him ;
and, doubting of his own worth and vali-
ance as a champion in the lists of love, he
fled from Paris in a fever of unrest, seeking
quiet and appeasement with relatives of
his Flemish mother at Fampoux, in the
Pas-de-Calais. Thence, breaking through
the strict rules of procedure approved by
French custom, he precipitately despatched

a complete avowal and prayer for marriage
to his friend Charles, who, with similar in-
correction, spoke directly of the proposal
to Mlle. Mathilde herself, and heartened
the love-sick Paul by bidding him hope for
a proper issue to his written pleading.
This was not long delayed, for the suitor
enjoyed a comfortable patrimony, and a
year later the marriage was celebrated
amid the excitement of disastrous war
and the rumour of Macmahon's first
defeat.

The war over, Verlaine, with a strange
and lamentable wrong-headedness, re-
frained from reporting himself to his
official chiefs after the troubled interreg-
num of the short-lived Commune, and so
lost his place. This piece of obstinate
negligence was due to unfounded fears lest
an unfavourable interpretation should be
put on his temporary absence during the
hazardous period of transition from the
monarchical to the republican regime. He
thus drifted into that life of aimless
dawdling which, for a man of his temperament, was, in itself, an invitation to
calamity. He was now installed with his

wife and her parents in the home of the
latter, and the squabbles between the
young pair became daily more frequent
and more bitter, for Verlaine, the mildest
of men when sober, became at once fretful
and querulous under the influence of
drink. He was at this time one of the
chosen frequenters of the *salon* of the eccen-
tric and vivacious Mme. Nina de Callias,
who joined together under her roof, in
the most unconventional good fellowship,
artists, writers, and dilettantes of every
kind. Daughter of a Lyons lawyer, separated from her husband—a brilliant but
unstable journalist addicted to absinthe—
chaperoned by her mother, the " sombre,
impassive, strange-looking Mme. Gaillard,
dressed always in mourning, and as though
unconscious, in the midst of our noisiest
hubbub, which she seemed not to hear,"
her lodging was long the resort of that
fighting advance guard of letters that was
then issuing from the slopes of the French
" *Parnasse,*" beneath the guiding arms of
Théodore de Banville and Léconte de
l'Isle. François Coppée, Léon Dierx, Ana-
tole France, Catulle Mendés, Albert Mérat,

might all have been met there, and lording
it among them all, like Lucifer among the
rebel angels, was the romantic and fas-
cinating figure of Villiers de l'Isle-Adam,
basking in the avid smiles of the hostess,
whose favoured lover he claimed to be.
The "*Fêtes Galantes*" of 1869, expressing
those "vagues et delicieuses confidences,
à mi voix, au crépuscule," that we associate
with the idylls of Watteau, is a direct
mirror of his original impressions of this
milieu.[1] But it was not one that was conducive to hearthstone virtues, and Lepelletier gives us an instructive account of an
after-supper ramble in the Bois-de-Bou-
logne and a murderous attack which Verlaine made upon him under the influence
of discussion and drink. Salvation was
sought by flight to a new *milieu* among
those hospitable Flemings of north-eastern
France from whom, on the maternal side,
he sprang.

"Smoke two pipes after dinner (at
12), drink seven or eight tumblers at

[1] A more facetious rendering is given by Mr. George
Moore in his "Memoirs of My Dead Life," in the section
entitled "Ninon's Table d'Hôte."

the inn (4 to 5), and watch the night-fall in the wood, while reading some book of a quieting kind—such is my new life, which differs from that down yonder."

So he wrote to an old Paris crony from the sugar factory of his cousin.

After some months spent in visiting relations and friends at Fampoux, Lécluse, and Arleux, the pair returned to Paris, and the growing incompatibility became at last intolerable. The final rupture came when, into a household already suffering from the emotional turmoils of reproaches and recriminations, was introduced the over-bearing, arrogant person of Arthur Rimbaud, who, by some kind of occult power, subdued Verlaine to his perverse will and held him captive. Ten years younger than Verlaine, and, like him, son of a military captain and an Ardennais, he had already thrice played truant from his home and sought hospitality in Paris, where he had arrived penniless, his sole endowment being complete belief in his own powers, combined with entire scorn for that of all

others—of all others, that is, save one, and
that one Paul Verlaine, at that time known
to him only as the author of " *Poèmes Saturniens.*" To him, as though impelled by some
atavistic presentiment, he had addressed
a letter of enthusiastic homage, accompanying some astounding lyric efforts of
his own, a bait which the simple Paul, un-
recognized, hankering after sympathy and
really impressed by the masterful origin-
ality of the manuscript submitted, so
readily swallowed that he wrote back with
equal warmth, summoning Rimbaud to
Paris as his guest. The youth arrived, un-
shaven, unkempt, silent and churlish ;
stubbornly irresponsive to the compliments
and well-meaning affability of his new
hosts, and, later on, as little grateful for
the successive kindnesses that were show-
ered on him by a long list of soft-hearted
Bohemians (among whom was the distin-
guished *Parnassien* de Banville) who gave
him either the shelter of their roof or the
tribute of their purses. So quarrelsome
and so insolent did he become that a
certain informal club of young penmen,
calling itself " Les Vilains Bonshommes,"

whose hospitality he had repaid with sharpest stabs of contradiction or surly dumbness, decided on his exclusion from their future gatherings. This action, though amply justified by an unseemly brawl due to Rimbaud's wanton aggression, offended Verlaine ; and, further relations with his wife having become impossible, he set out on an aimless wandering from Paris to the Nord, and thence by way of Belgium, across the Channel to London, in company with his evil and tyrannous familiar.

> " Ah, wasteful woman, she who may
>   On her sweet self set her own price,
> Knowing man cannot choose but pay,
>   How has she cheapen'd paradise."

So sang Coventry Patmore in " The Angel in the House." But, whatever reproaches Madame Paul Verlaine may have deserved, this is not one of them : she set her price, and that was temperance, and what would have followed therefrom, respect for herself as wife and mother of the son but newly born to them. Verlaine could not pay it, could not wean himself from his cups and the sinister influence of Rimbaud, a youth who openly held all fixed occupations in abhorrence, and hankered, as did Keats, but less healthily than he, for a life of pure sensation, unfettered by moral obligations or material needs.

IV

EARLY one July morning in 1872, Verlaine
and Rimbaud took train for Arras, where
they arrived early, and repaired forthwith
to the refreshment-bar. Many glasses
soon made them talkative, and the satanic
Rimbaud, giving rein to that morbid relish
which became him as the avowed wor-
shipper of sacrilege, set about scandalizing
his hearers with tales of robbery, murder,
and sudden death, in which he nonchal-
antly professed himself a direct participant.
Verlaine at once took up the cue, posing
gravely as an accomplice in the blackest of
crimes and a fugitive from avenging justice.
Word was quickly carried to the local
police, and two constables soon appeared
on the scene, inviting the tipsy travellers
to follow them. Search and inquiry at
the police station soon revealed that the
authorities had been hoaxed, and the note
of apology having been sounded, Verlaine

promptly produced all the necessary *pièces justificatives,* and fell headlong into a tirade of abuse and menace for the indignity of having been wrongly accused and detained. But for this ill-timed and senseless outburst, at the close of a predicament entirely self-created, the pair would doubtless have been free to go forward without further molestation ; but Verlaine drunk was a reckless being stirring up hornets' nests that gave him ample stings to spur remorse and self-pity in Verlaine sober. As it was, they were conducted back to the railway station and placed in the next train returning to Paris. Arrived there they immediately set out direct for Belgium, whence they crossed to London. Thence Verlaine sent many letters to the loyal Lepelletier, giving his impressions of the London streets, their shops, bars, bootblacks, and intolerable Sundays, all viewed with a superficial eye, but set down with great vivacity and point, though mainly distorted from the standpoint of a dweller on the northern outskirts of Soho with a hankering after the salacious. Thence he also sent home for publication the verses

entitled " *Les Amies*," a poetical apotheosis of the Lesbian which was promptly
confiscated by the police, in the wise exercise of a power in itself arbitrary. Meanwhile his wife was actively engaged in
seeking a separation in the law courts,
and Verlaine's counsel as actively oppos-
ing it, the truant husband stubbornly deny-
ing the charge of perverse intimacy with
his companion Rimbaud, which was the
main ground of his wife's plea. Lepelletier throughout his biography never ceases
to proclaim Verlaine as innocent of the
charge, but the most indulgent verdict
that an open-minded judge could possibly
return would be that of " Not Proven ";
while both Verlaine's antecedents and his
subsequent history, to say nothing of the
internal evidence of his work and of his
correspondence, point insistently to the
probability of his guilt. Though he had
done nothing to avert suspicion and everything likely to arouse it, Verlaine, throughout, denounced the proceedings as the out-
come of a conspiracy prompted by his wife's
parents, and aided by forgery and false
witness, the latter being specially directed,

as he supposed, to proving his complicity in the events of the Commune. Giving a general power of attorney to the faithful Lepelletier (himself the object of suspicion for his inopportune political views), he did his best to forget his troubles in studying the vagaries of shady frequenters in Soho, whom he describes with his usual candour. It was arranged that Rimbaud should return to his home at Charleville, and that Verlaine's mother should join him in London, where, firmly turning his back on past disasters, he was to begin life anew. He seems to have been absurdly oversanguine. " Living is a hundred times cheaper than at Paris, the climate a hundred times more healthy, and work infinitely easier to find."

Rimbaud's departure was followed by an illness so severe that he expressed his despair of surviving, and telegraphed, in his extremity, for his wife, his mother, and his friend. The two latter promptly obeyed his summons, and nursed him back to strength. Once restored, they again left the exile, his mother counselling his return to France, or at least to Belgium, where he would be beyond the reach of French jurisdiction—though for what offence against it he had to fear reprisal Lepelletier does not explain. He crossed over the Channel, and settled with an aunt at Jéhonville in the Belgian portion of Luxembourg, in the hope that his wife would consent to interview him there, and that a reconciliation might ensue from their meeting. This sudden veering of his intentions is symptomatic both of his growing infirmity of purpose, and of that childish self-deception that shows, in nearness of mocking mirage, the thing sought by the thirsting seeker whose great desire creates its own shadow without the substance of fulfilment. He seems to have been very happy and hopeful during this period. The association which had caused his wife's imputations had been broken ; he was assured at least that his wife's obduracy was not prompted by another attachment ; and the pastoral calm served to allay that excitability which might have been too easily ruffled and appeased in the mean streets of cosmopolitan Soho. He ate trout with the country priest, " divine clerical trout" taken from the "black river on a bed of chattering pebbles"; he wandered in the woods alone or with the unspoilt country folk of his father's kindred, with whom, as a boy, he had passed so many happy summers. On the darker side, we have to note that he writes to Lepelletier of a cerebral crisis which had overwhelmed him at Namur, begging him to say nothing of the matter to his mother. But a month's stay was enough to convince him how irrevocable was the decision which his wife had taken, all his overtures for her return being promptly repulsed in the most unequivocal terms. There is no doubt that, while here, he made efforts to achieve sobriety and regular living. He planned a series of pastoral poems, that was to follow the "*Romances sans paroles*" which he now entrusted to Lepelletier for publication, insisting that the volume should be dedicated to Rimbaud as a token of gratitude for his devotion during the illness above cited. But Verlaine's righteousness, in order to persist, needed assurance of a rewarding heaven, and the gates on that having been fast locked by his unrelenting wife, it is to be feared that his self-reclamation thereafter became little more than histrionic, though the spark of aspiration still hovered unquenched in his wayward soul.

V

AFTER two months spent at Jéhonville, Verlaine set out once more for the "Fog's City," as he facetiously termed the British capital. The motive of this return is not explained, and we are left to infer that the charm of country life had gradually dissolved into dullness for a curiosity that was avid of sensation and a mind that was dependent on material stimulants for its illumination.

"I am giving French lessons," he writes from Camden Town, in June, 1873. "That brings me in something like five or six pounds a month." The wish in this case was probably father to the thought, for at this date he can hardly have had more than a fortnight's experience on which to base his estimate.[1] Were it true, it would prove his exceeding good luck in a very pre-

---

[1] Rimbaud gives twelve francs a week as the probable income of their combined teaching.

carious calling, especially when we remember his slender qualifications, and his very casual way of drifting into it.

Whether Rimbaud rejoined him by invitation or at his own prompting we do not know. Lepelletier prints no word of Verlaine which might suggest anticipation of his return ; but the same month Rimbaud was back with him in London, and living, as usual, at his friend's expense. Quarrels were frequent, and Verlaine suddenly embarked for Antwerp, without either warning his companion or leaving for him the means of continuing alone. This would seem to point to the conclusion that Rimbaud had sought reunion against Verlaine's wish, and that the latter had resolved on breaking away from his disastrous influence.

He wrote from Brussels begging his mother and his wife to join him, but only the older woman appeared, as he might well have foreseen. Overwhelmed once more by the apparent hopelessness of regaining the esteem of the wife for whom he still seems to have cherished a worshipping fondness, and, perhaps thinking that if,

socially, he were to die, he might as well be
killed for a wolf as for a lamb, he gave way
to another bout of drinking, and despatched
a penitent telegram to Rimbaud, praying
him to forgive and return. Rimbaud lost
no time in doing so, but seems to have
been no longer eager to resume the strange
ménage à deux founded on a friendship
so brittle. He projected a visit to Paris, and
demanded the means from Verlaine, growing furious and threatening on its refusal.
It would appear that Verlaine, exasperated
by Rimbaud's peremptory demand for
money, and his firm decision to abandon
him on receiving it, fired two revolver
shots, one of which slightly wounded his
pensioner on the left wrist. Poor Mère
Verlaine thereupon intervened, and Verlaine, overborne by remorse, begged Rimbaud to take the weapon and render
justice on himself, the wretched aggressor.
The passionate apology was at once ac-
cepted, the wound staunched, and the sum
of twenty pounds handed to the victim
for the immediate return to Charleville, on
which he declared himself resolved. But, as
the pair were on their way to the station,

Rimbaud (without cause, as Verlaine maintained) took fright at signs of a further attempt to fire on him, and rushed across the street crying loudly for help. Verlaine was promptly arrested and consigned to prison on a charge of attempted murder, while Rimbaud, waiting a few days for the healing of his wound and the preferment of his charge, went on his way in calm security to Charleville. A month later Verlaine was found guilty and sentenced to two years' imprisonment. The seclusion that followed at Mons, and the enforced calm and frugality of the wholesome, if heartless, prison routine, was, perhaps, the happiest period, subsequent to a spoilt childhood, that the poet ever knew. His conversion, while bringing home to his irresponsible soul the sad unthrift of his rudderless wanderings, and the guilt of his enslavement to the joys of sense, gave a depth of feeling, and—despite the mystical nature of his theme—greater clarity to the record of it that was later to be issued under the title of " *Sagesse*." The " sense of sin " has never found intenser utterance or more sincere than in the celebrated sonnet recording his dread of the "*faux beaux jours.*"

Les faux beaux jours ont lui tout le jour, ma pauvre âme,
Et les voici vibrer aux cuivres du couchant.
Ferme les yeux, pauvre âme, at rentre sur-le-champ :
Une tentation des pires.   Fuis l'infâme.

Ils ont lui tout le jour en longs grêlons de flammes
Battant toute vendange aux collines, couchant
Toute moisson de la vallée, et ravageant
Le ciel tout bleu, le ciel chanteur qui te réclame.

O palis, et va-t'en, lente et joignant les mains.
Si ces hiers allaient manger nos beaux demains ?
Si la vieille folie était encore en route ?

Ces souvenirs, va-t-il falloir les retuer ?
Un assaut furieux, le suprême, sans doute !
O, va prier contre l'orage, va prier.

But he was to decline from such music to the composition of *billets* to the filthiest of slatterns.

VI

LEPELLETIER, unable to find a publisher
willing to act as sponsor for the " *Romances
sans paroles*," owing to the ill-fame of their
author, resolved on publishing the volume
himself, and this was done at Sens, to
which city he had retired for the continu-
ance of " *Le Peuple Souverain*," a republican journal which had been suppressed in
Paris by order of the military governor.
Five hundred copies were printed, and,
though the work was not issued for sale,
copies were sent for review to the leading
publications, and to the leading writers,
whose goodwill and opinion Verlaine valued.
At Verlaine's express wish a copy was sent
to his wife, but no acknowledgment was
returned, and the appeal which he had
made to her in " Birds in the Night " remained without answer. Among the several
copies sent to London friends, was one in-
tended for Swinburne, with whom per-

sonally, however, the author was not acquainted. Of the papers thus circularized not one even cited the book's title among its publications received, and but two or three among some fifty personal recipients deigned to grant the author their thanks for his gift. At Paris, Victor Hugo, besought by the despairing poet on the eve of his trial, though personally unknown to him, had unsuccessfully petitioned for a remission of Verlaine's sentence. The prisoner persisted in hoping for a reconciliation with his wife, whom he pictured as overwhelmed with remorse for the disasters which he imputed to her having failed him in his need, but still too overpowered by paternal influence to dare a declaration of unshaken fidelity and her resolve to return to him.

He was now full of a project of writing for the stage on his release, and there is ample evidence that he possessed a vein of loose satire well suited to the demands of ephemeral vaudeville. His mother visited him, and, thanks to her bounty, a provision of special food reached him daily from the prison kitchens, and letters were smuggled through to Lepelletier without having first passed the eyes of the official censor. Enforced idleness drove him seriously to the study of English authors, several of whom were represented in the prison library ; he even thought of translation as a source of regular income, named several books which he proposed to bring forward in French garb, and completed a version of a " delicious short story " by Dickens, of which the title is not given, and of which we have no further record. " There are at London," he writes, " a crowd of worthy writers full of talent, quite unknown in France, and who would eagerly welcome the chance of being rendered into our idiom." He still held to the possibility of resuming his post at the Hôtel de Ville at Paris. " After all," he writes, " I am neither a deserter nor a communard, like several we know who are quietly scribbling reports at this moment. And as to my imprisonment, there is nothing, I flatter myself, dishonourable about it, and it is, above all, a misfortune, but a reparable one, I believe." The Paris courts evidently viewed his condemnation more seriously, and granted his wife's suit for a separation. The news of this drove all hope from his mind, and annihilated for the moment all his various plans of future work. Bereft thus of all encouragement from outer sources, there was left nothing but the world of inward vision and suggestion to console him. His conversion rapidly followed. It was doubtless mainly brought about by the forced abandonment of his old habits, and his *moral* conversion was to be found wanting when he was once more free to renew them. But so long as he was in the right *milieu* to support him there can be no doubt that his conversion was not only sincere, but effective. His penitence was without a shadow of the histrionic, for, indeed, there was no gallery to applaud him, as was afterwards unhappily the case in those deplorable last days when the cult of his poetry became confused with the ill living of its maker, as though that had been the mainspring which was, in fact, only a symptom of the overpowering nervous sensibility to which both were due. He was even afraid to speak openly of his religious experiences and convictions to Lepelletier, for fear of the latter's misunderstanding and ridicule. Sending him " *Sagesse* " he writes: "It is absolutely heartfelt, I assure you. You must have gone through all that I have suffered the last three years, humiliation, disdain, insult, in order to realize how admirably consoling, reasonable, logical is this religion, so terrible and so gentle. Oh! terrible. Yes! but man is so evil, so truly fallen, and punished by his birth alone; I do not speak of historical, scientific, or other proofs, which are overwhelming, when there is this stupendous happiness of being withdrawn from the abominable society of the rotten and the aged, of dolts, snobs, and the damned." The sentiment hardly sounds Christian in spite of its occasion.

On the 16th January, 1875, he was released, having earned a slight remission for good conduct during detention. His mother awaited him at the prison entrance, and the two set out at once for Arras and Fampoux, and thence, after a short period of quiet with old friends, to Paris. A flying visit was paid to Stuttgart, where Rimbaud was now installed as French tutor in a doctor's family, and from this fact it would seem that Verlaine's infatuation was left unaffected by his religious translation. The legend goes that he was ill received, his attempts at conversion repulsed, and himself abandoned insensible after an angry encounter in the Black Forest. The elder man, thrown over by the strong, audacious nature on which he had learnt to lean for the support and inspiration now impatiently refused him, returned to Paris, and the two were never again to meet. But Verlaine, in whom the force of conversion was not yet spent—" of all men of genius I have ever met," says George Moore, " the least fitted to defend himself in the battle of life "—realized the danger of the capital to a man of his tendencies left uncompanioned, and sought by advertisement a place *au pair* in an English boarding-school, which, after a month's delay, was found him at Stickney, near Boston, in Lincolnshire. He must be accounted fortunate in having found so prompt and comfortable a refuge ; but it was to prove no more than a rut in the long road along which, like the dead leaf of his fancy, he was to drift before the untempered wind of circumstance.

> Les sanglots longs
> Des violons
>   De l'automne
> Blessent mon cœur
> D'une langueur
>   Monotone.
>
> Tout suffocant
> Et blême, quand
>   Sonne l'heure,
> Je me souviens
> Des jours anciens
>   Et je pleure ;
>
> Et je m'en vais
> Au vent mauvais
>   Qui m'emporte
> Deçà, delà
> Pareil à la
>   Feuille morte.

He was introduced to his pupils, by their principal, in the following words, which seem to veil a threat of which we may say very truly that " the sting is in the tail."

" Monsieur Verlaine, who is a Bachelor of Arts of the University of Paris, is willing to assist me in teaching the French language and the art of drawing. He knows English as well as an Englishman, and most certainly far better than all of you put together, but, of course, he cannot pronounce it . . . quite well. I am convinced that you will respect and like this gentleman. But should any of you take advantage of his foreign accent to show him the least want of respect, I shall lose no time in . . . correcting the error."

VII

" DEAR friend," he writes (10th April, 1876)
to Lepelletier, from his new home, " Behold
me, teacher on mutual terms, in an English
village. No one around me speaks a word
of French, not a traitor word. I teach
French, Latin . . . and drawing ! I get
through these duties well enough. And I
teach in English, which is, above all, extraordinary. What English ! but after
eight days here, I am improving.

" Home life. Mr. Andrews is a young
man who reads French as I read English,
but who doesn't speak it. . . . Zuze !
For the rest, charming, cordial, well
educated." And again: " I have no dis-
tractions and seek none. Immense reading, walks with pupils (not in rank, you
know, no herding here) across the magnifi-
cent meadows, full of sheep, etc. For a
week past, it has been wonderful how well
I have felt, both morally and physically."

He was again benefiting from the influence
of a wholesome and strict regime, and the
still greater influence of kind people who
thought well of him, and whose belief he
would not wish to belie. But after eighteen
months here, occupied in quiet and steady
work in which poetry played small part,
home-sickness, or " reasons which I only
vaguely remember," as he wrote in the
" Fortnightly Review " in 1894, drove him
once again to Arras, where his mother rejoined him. Here he resumed his versify-
ing and revised " *Sagesse,*" but suddenly,
without motive given, we hear of his return
to Boston, not, however, to his former post,
but as a private teacher. According to
his own record, just quoted, his mother
now accompanied him and they lodged
together in Boston. His private pupils
included a German who had fought at
Sedan, to whom, as to his teacher, English
was a secondary and most difficult medium
of speech. Pupils failing him, he sought a
mastership, and was appointed to a private
school at Bournemouth, where he continued
adding to the pieces that were to appear
in " *Sagesse,*" and where his health was

doubtlessly improved by his daily bathing in the sea. But his stay here was still shorter than at Stickney; and, following a brief visit to Paris, we find him, in the autumn of 1878, installed as teacher of literature, history, geography, and English in the Roman Catholic College of Notre-Dame at Rethel, in his ancestral country of the Ardennes, where most of his colleagues on the school staff were priests. He wrote cheerfully to Lepelletier of his life here, but forbade him to inform anyone of his address. Punctual, pious, taciturn seem to be the adjectives best suited to his conduct here, so far as it could be observed by his associates, by whom both his past history and his accomplishment as a poet were entirely unguessed. But his stay here hardly outlasted a full cycle of the seasons; for, having conceived a deep attachment for one of his pupils, Lucien Létinois, a country lad of nineteen, he resigned his post in order to taste the pleasures of farm-life on the homestead occupied by the parents of his young idol.

Lepelletier attributes this affection to the baulked paternal instinct of Verlaine, and, in so doing, is only following the latter's own interpretation as witnessed repeatedly in his book "*Amour*." Whatever the motive, the attraction, as in the case of Rimbaud, was a disastrous one, for it lured him away from a life of settled security and profitable diligence, to the same aimless wandering that had already proved his undoing. He now bought a farm where his mother and his boy friend joined him, ownership being vested in the latter's father, for no clearer reason than Verlaine's professed fear of future claims on it from his wife, now legally separated and soon to be divorced. The would-be farmer did not prosper, and one morning the nominal owner found it deserted, the poet having set out for his old haunts with his new companion. The father, very naturally, sold the estate for his own profit, and the proceeds were another loss to the private income which, steadily shrinking since the death of Captain Verlaine, was ultimately to leave the poet on the verge of destitution. Lack of money soon drove Verlaine back across Channel to Paris, where he settled with Létinois on the out-

skirts of the famous *Bois* at Paris, on the
tireless bounty of his good mother, then
resident at Boulogne. There he made in-
effectual efforts to regain the post at the
Hôtel de Ville, of which his own negligence
and indiscretion had deprived him some
eight years earlier. "*Sagesse*" was pub-
lished, but its appearance attracted no
attention.

His bosom friend was stricken with
typhoid fever and succumbed. "*Amour*,"
which celebrates the apotheosis of this
friendship, and gives cause for our assuming it to have been of the nobler sort,
echoes also the accents of a heartfelt grief
for this dire visitation of God's judgment—
to use the expression which best reflects
the author's manner of viewing his misfortune. We may note that he writes of
his love as "*paternelle vraiment*," and of
the lad as "*mon fils*," thus giving to his
attachment that higher sanction which
Lepelletier claims for it.

VIII

In 1880 Lepelletier, then editor-in-chief of the " *Réveil,*" a popular daily, gave Verlaine a staff position on his paper, and encouraged him to write a series of sketches, mainly autobiographical (as was all that Verlaine ever touched in prose), which appeared under the heading of " *Paris-Vivant.*" Later they were to appear with others in the collection entitled " *Les Mémoires d'un veuf,*" lively, facetious, garrulous, but seldom ill-humoured chatter about his past vicissitudes, or the scenes of his present wanderings by *boulevard* or *banlieue*. They contain also a rather grandiloquent definition of the mission of poetry, which was very likely sincere when written. "Above all arts, of which she is the eldest, and of which she remains the queen, she shrinks from moral ugliness." The volume contains also a lampoon on Victor Hugo, marked with all the unbridled fury of iconoclasm, which seems unforgivable when we consider the goodwill and practical effort of the great bard on behalf of an unknown singer when in misfortune. In this Lepelletier says that Verlaine was insincere, that at heart he never lost his profound reverence for the master, but was spurred on to the attack by the crowd of young hopefuls whom he was already " receiving " daily over the marble slab of a café table. From this point onwards in Verlaine's career, it becomes more and more difficult to distinguish between the serious artist and the deplorable *cabotin* continually cheated of that inner approval of his higher artistic conscience by his relish for tickling the groundlings to applause. " *Les Poètes Maudits*" soon appeared with the imprint of Léon Vanier, a publisher to whom Verlaine had become known through young associates of the Latin Quarter, among whom henceforward he was to be dispenser of poetic law and patronage. Without the least rancour, he gives a generous appraisal of Rimbaud, whose extraordinary " *Voyelles*," a sonnet attributing a fixed value of colour suggestion

to each of the vowel sounds, he quotes in
full, as also the not less remarkable " *Cher-
cheuses de Poux,*" whose questing, to yield
beauty, must surely be taken in that
symbolic way which was later to provide a
justification, if also something of an
apology, for the methods of his school.
Tristan Corbière, Stéphane Mallarmé, Villiers de l'Isle-Adam, and the " Pauvre
Lelian "[1] himself (justifying his poetry of
the profaner sensations on the score of a
sincerity equal when felt to that born of
the religious impulse), complete a very
mixed company for the meek vestal
Marceline Désbordes-Valmore who appears
among them. He would seem now to have
had his foot on the first rung of the ladder
to literary success, and had added a
volume of verse " *Jadis et Naguère* " to the
manuscript entrusted to Vanier for publication. But suddenly revisited by his
hankering for the life bucolic, arising, no
doubt unconsciously, from a healthy bodily
need for exercise and renewal, he left Paris,

---

[1] An anagram on *Paul Verlaine* in which he disguised
his own name and by which he was thereafter widely
known.

without warning to friends or any motive assigned, and settled in the neighbourhood of Rheims, hard by the site of his former failure as a tiller of the soil. He had induced his mother to buy a house at Coulommes from the parents of his lost Lucien. As before, the enterprise failed lamentably from Verlaine's obvious unfitness and the want of a strong hand to keep him straight. Debts accumulated and the *cabaret* found in him a too profitable frequenter whose orgies soon became the scandal of his fellow villagers. Money began to run short, and Verlaine bled his mother unmercifully for the means to indulge his insatiable thirst. She made over the property to him, perhaps with a view to escaping responsibility for its debts ; and, worn out by incessant bickering and the outrageous exactions of the uncontrollable drunkard, decided at seventy-five years of age that she was justified in leaving him and seeking shelter under the roof of a neighbour named Dane. On the 9th February, 1885, Verlaine came to Paris, possibly to consult with Vanier about the publication of "*Jadis et Naguère*," but more probably driven by the demon of

unrest, and pondering a return to England,
his usual asylum whenever he fell foul of
the world about him. Two days later,
however, irresolute as ever, he was back
again at Coulommes, perhaps hoping that
the inexhaustible good nature of his mother
would have led her to return. Disappointed
in this hope, he turned to the house of M.
Dane, with anger and resentment whipped
up to boiling point by the usual surflux of
strong drink. A scene ensued in which Verlaine, with physical violence, attempted to
obtain further supplies from his mother,
and accompanied the aggression, knife in
hand, with threats of death. Despite all
Lepelletier's special pleading on his behalf
there can be little doubt of Verlaine's un-
extenuated guilt on this charge, for we can
find no grounds for imputing personal ill-
will to M. Dane, and without his insistent
efforts to protect an aged woman indulgent
to the point of stupidity, a still direr
calamity would very probably have come
to pass. It was with difficulty that she
was now induced to testify against her son ;
all her evidence is compact of fond excuses :
he had, as ever, been led away by evil

companions; he was a good son when
sober; he had never ill-used or threatened
her before, and so on. Poor victim as he
was of those inherent weaknesses and col-
lusive circumstances that are beyond the
power of any man's choosing, he was yet
lucky in receiving no more than a month's
imprisonment as reprisal for this murderous
aggression.

Verlaine was liberated on the 13th May,
1885. Just before his trial he had sold in
haste the house at Coulommes for 1300
francs less than his mother had paid for it
a year before, and now had no real home to
which to go. He returned to Paris a con-
firmed dipsomaniac, self-indulgence and
the want of any corrective physical activity
being punished by a growing muscular
numbness, with which self-control (or the
lack of it) is so nearly allied. Alternating
between bars and hospitals, an easy prey
to outworn harpies of the Boulevards, a
dupe to the adulations of callow and
rebellious youth, the closing years of Verlaine's life provide a spectacle which can
only make the judicious grieve.

IX

"*Jadis et Naguère*" now appeared, and Verlaine sought the good offices of the indefatigable Lepelletier for the purposes of log-rolling. This volume contains some of Verlaine's finest work, though interlaced with many early experiments and imitations, the salvage of his young years which he was now tempted to issue, in view of the apparent exhaustion of his original creative vein. He seems never to have forgotten an occasion of the making of verses, and carefully husbanded every scrap, however indifferent in quality or unfitted for publication ; and from this fact his publisher derived much profit, while burdening Verlaine with a reputation for much work far below his best, and little worthy of the Muse's trafficking. "*Les Uns et Les Autres*," a series of Watteau-like scenes, was produced in 1891 through the enterprise of Paul Fort, the present wearer, following Léon Dierx, of Verlaine's laurels in that dynasty of Poet Princes elected by the oncoming novitiates of song. The performance did no more than pay for its expenses, to the great disappointment and passing spleen of the author, for whose benefit and that of the painter Gauguin it had been organized.

Atritic rheumatism, the tendency to which he had inherited from his father, now drove Verlaine to seek treatment in the many hospitals that were to shelter him during these latter years. He was bedridden in the unfloored room of a hovel behind a low-class wine-shop when he heard, in January, 1886, of his mother's death, and wrote to Lepelletier, in the first flush of his remorseful sorrow, to come and cheer him. The change from such a lodging to the cleanliness and simple comfort of public institutions was a benefit of which he was gratefully aware, and the forced sobriety and diligence which followed his entrance to them prove how little he was fit for life in the outer millpool of the world, and how well he might have done in that cloistral seclusion where his temperament and constitution could alone

find strength and security. The ardent
spark of his spirit was like a flame within a
lamp wherein alone it can aspire, but which
any sudden inlet of the outer air must
flutter to extinction. So these periods of
enforced calm seem in the event only to
have served as a whetstone to the edge of
an appetite blunted by past surfeiting,
and despite all resolutions, his release was
always an occasion for further orgies. In
the too few and too brief moments of
sobriety his self-respect would burn fiercely
within him. Then, forgetting that his own
loose ways and too pliant pen were to
blame for the survival of ill legends con-
cerning him, he would turn and rend the
applauders who had betrayed him.

Rompons ! Ce que j'ai dit je ne le reprends pas.
Puisque je le pensai c'est donc que c'était vrai.
Je le garderai, jusqu'au jour ou je mourrai,
Total, intégral, pur, en dépit des combats,

De la rancour très haute et de l'orgeuil très bas.
Mais comme un fier metal qui sort du minerai
De vos nuages à la fin je surgirai,
Je surgis, amities d'ennuis et de débats. . . .

O pour l'affection toute simple et si douce
Ou l'âme se blottit comme en un nid de mousse !
Et fi donc de la sale " âme parisienne " !

PAUL VERLAINE

Vive l'ésprit français, d'Artois jusqu'en Gascogne
De la Champagne et de l'Argonne à la Bourgogne
Et vive un cœur, morbleu ! dont un cœur se souvienne !

Meanwhile his divorced wife had now re-married, his request for a visit from his son, now a lad of fifteen, had been refused by her, and his whole available fortune had shrunk to something like two hundred and fifty pounds. Despite this gloomy commentary on his past failures, he writes from his second hospital to Lepelletier, still nursing the unconquerable hope of a steady income from steady work on recovery. But disappearance followed his release, suggesting only too surely a return to his cups and a further postponement of all creative effort. Six months later he is back again in his first hospital, cheered somewhat by the fillip given to his reputation by the republication of the several volumes that had issued stillborn from the press ten or more years before, but finding his fame almost barren of pecuniary reward. He talked of a return to his English teaching for a livelihood, of a grant that was being solicited in his favour from the Ministry of Education, and of further contributions to journalism. But his resolutions of industry quickly evaporated in the free air of independence and the bright allure of the hospitable café tables. Lepelletier tried to persuade him away from Paris, as his guest at Bougival, where, as a friendly overseer, he hoped to forestall the invalid's too easy backsliding. Verlaine began to feel the reproach of his poverty, and to suspect the condescension of charity in those who were succouring him, and he now expressed himself ready to join Lepelletier, and to submit himself to a sober and diligent regime ; but his illness still kept him in the hospitals, and when finally he was able to quit them for a while, this unwearied friend was unable to save him from a prompt resumption of his deplorable ways.

He fell once more under the unprofitable influence of the adulating Latin Quarter, to which " *Parallèlement*," which he now issued, must be largely attributed. This is a collection of verses mainly in daring laud of carnal gluttony, eked out with pieces full of sportive verbal sleight not without a spice of self-mockery. Much of it no doubt has genuine delight, but as much again only a feigned relish in these obscene buffooneries. He now went to Aix-les-Bains for a cure, and how much of the histrionic could enter into Verlaine's compositions of this type, is revealed by his letter thence to the young artist Cazals, now his favoured crony, proposing to concoct a gross rendering of his lament for Lucien Létinois, as a likely bait for the eager mouths of his salacious admirers. He had lost something of the compunction of which he had still been capable in " *Sagesse* " :—

Beauté des femmes, leur faiblesse, et ces mains pâles
Qui font souvent le bien et peuvent tout le mal.
Et ces yeux, où plus rien ne reste d'animal
Que juste assez pour dire : "assez" aux fureurs mâles.

Et toujours, maternelle endormeuse des râles,
Même quand elle ment, cette voix ! Matinal
Appel, ou chant bien doux à vêpre, ou frais signal,
Ou beau sanglot qui va mourir au pli des châles !

Hommes durs ! Vie atroce et laide d'ici-bas !
Ah ! que, du moins, loin des baisers et des combats,
Quelque chose demeure un peu sur la montagne,

Quelque chose du cœur enfantin et subtil,
Bonté, respect ! Car qu'est ce qui nous accompagne,
Et vraiment, quand la mort viendra, que resta-t-il ?

He soon returned to Paris and to hospital, there hugging the grievance of his lack of success with the daily papers, for which, to an onlooker, his work is seen to have been so little suitable. " I am not a beggar," he wrote, " I am a well-known man of letters, and nearly dying of hunger "—" of thirst " the undazzled onlooker is tempted to retort.

He seems to have been well liked, both as patient and as fellow-inmate of the various hospitals that sheltered him, and his contentment when under treatment has been witnessed by Mr. Arthur Symons :—

" I have never seen so cheerful an invalid as he used to be at that hospital, the Hôpital Saint-Louis, where at one time I used to go and see him every week. His whole face seemed to chuckle as he would tell me, in his emphatic, confiding way, everything that entered into his head ; the droll stories cut short by a groan, a lamentation, a sudden fury of reminiscence, at which his face would cloud or convulse, the wild eyebrows slanting up and down ; and then suddenly, the good laugh would be back, clearing the air."

PAUL VERLAINE

In the spring of 1891 Verlaine had come as near a complete cure as was possible to one of his constitution and habits, and bade a grateful farewell to the institution which had brought it about. He returned to the Latin Quarter, to the solace of the cabarets and the care of heartless viragoes who bartered their fading charms against the possibilities of his uncertain earnings—and alms.

X

" LIVING in thieves' quarters, getting drunk, writing beautiful poems in the hospitals, coming out of hospitals and falling in love with drabs,"[1] the closing years of Verlaine's life were passed in lamentable indigence and ill-health. Whatever money he acquired flowed away like water at the bars, and any surplus was promptly appropriated by the harpies to whom he had become a prey. There is little to admire and much to deplore in the poetical output of this last steep passage on the downward slope towards extinction. The lack of money goaded him into bartering unworthy " copy " for the satisfaction of his needs, his drawers were ransacked, and every scrap of rhyme—ribald, satiric, personal, and obscene—was dressed up in type, with a fine surplus of dedications

---

[1] George Moore.

which bear witness to the beggary of his independence.

He thought, and without laughing, of soliciting a *Fauteuil* among the forty immortals of the French Academy, to which his talent certainly entitled him, but was dissuaded by Lepelletier, who urged, quite frankly, his obvious unfitness for election as a member of the body politic. His " Wednesdays " became celebrated, and many devoted friends helped him by public insistence on the imperishable in his work, as well as by a privy untying of their purse-strings.

He was persuaded to give a series of lectures in Holland and Belgium, and, though he was only a poor speaker, and read his discourses, the result put some money into his pocket. Shortly after his return from this lecturing tour, he was introduced to Mr. Edmund Gosse, who, in his " French Profiles," gives a vivid and amusing picture of the manner in which the timid poet was run to earth, in a café of the Latin Quarter, by a party of admiring friends headed by the neo-classic, Jean Moréas. " Where I sat, by the elbow of

M. Moréas, I was opposite an open door, absolutely dark, leading down, by oblique stairs, to a cellar. As I idly watched this square of blackness I suddenly saw some ghostly shape fluttering at the bottom of it. It took the form of a strange bald head, bobbing close to the ground. Although it was so dim and vague, an idea crossed my mind. Not daring to speak, I touched M. Moréas, and so drew his attention to it. ' Pas un mot, pas un geste, Monsieur ! ' he whispered, and then, instructed in the guile of his race, *insidias Danaum*, the eminent author of ' *Les Catilènes* ' rose, making a vague detour towards the street, and then plunged at the cellar door. There was a prolonged scuffle and a rolling downstairs ; then M. Moréas reappeared, triumphant ; behind him something flopped up out of the darkness like an owl—a timid, shambling figure in a soft black hat, with jerking hands, and it peeped with intention to disappear again. But there were cries of ' Venez donc, Maître,' and by and by Verlaine was persuaded to emerge definitely and to sit by me.

" I had been prepared for strange eccen-

tricities of garb, but he was very decently
dressed; he referred at once to the fact,
and explained that this was the suit which
had been bought for him to lecture in, in
Belgium. He was particularly proud of a
real white shirt; ' C'est ma chemise de
conférence,' he said, and shot out the cuffs
of it with pardonable pride. He was full of
his experiences of Belgium, and in particular he said some very pretty things about
Bruges and its *béguinages*, and how much
he should like to spend the rest of his life
there. Yet it seemed less the medieval
buildings which had attracted him than a
museum of old lace. He spoke with a veiled
utterance, difficult for me to follow. Not
for an instant would he take off his hat, so
that I could not see the Socratic dome of
forehead which figures in all the caricatures.
I thought his countenance very Chinese,
and I may perhaps say here that when he
was in London, in 1894, I called him a
Chinese philosopher. He replied, ' Chinois
—comme vous voulez, mais philosophe—
non pas ! ' "

He came once more to London (1894)
where also he lectured, as the guest of Mr.

PAUL VERLAINE

Arthur Symons, his chief artistic disciple in England, to whom we owe the masterly appraisal of his work contained in " The Symbolist Movement." " I was amazed," writes his host, " by the exactitude of his memory of the mere turnings of the streets, the shapes and colours of the buildings, which he had not seen for twenty years." He wrote thence to his mistress, Eugénie Krantz, an offer of marriage, which seems the last thing one would have expected of him. He was doubtless, however, realizing that his physical force was nigh spent, that domestic comfort and security must at last replace philandering and vagabondage, and Eugénie was an excellent manager who knew how to take care of the pence.

" Do you speak seriously of marriage ? " he writes to her. " If yes, you will have won for me the greatest pleasure of my life ! We will go to the Mayor's whenever you will. It is moreover the surest way of getting you a fixed pension on my death. My darling ! Yes, that has always been my idea ! I love you only, and how much ! . . ." And again : " Your wishes are mine ; I know too well what it cost me to go

against you ; you are always right. . . .
Soon, dear wife, I kiss you and love you
with all my heart ! ''

Eugénie, according to Lepelletier, was
but indifferent honest, and light-heartedly
unobservant of any claims the poet may
have had on her fidelity ; but the marriage
was never to be celebrated.

On quitting one of his hospitals he had
sometimes found Philomène awaiting him,
sometimes Eugénie, or perhaps a third.
The first named was gentle and sisterly,
and spoke with an accent redolent of the
Nord, which had become endeared to him
by early associations. But she was legally
the wife of another, besides being shadowed
by the bully with whom she now shared
the spoils of conquest ; and so, with in-
terruptions, sordid squabbles and joyous
pardonings, Eugénie, though a shrew, a
niggard, and illiterate, was finally preferred, and reigned undisputed until his
death.

She had been one of the most celebrated
of the purchasable beauties who had
thronged boulevard and dancing-hall at the
close of the Second Empire, and in the long

succession of her fond victims she claimed among others of distinction the great Gambetta. At the time of her encounter with Verlaine she had long been ousted from the court of Venus by younger rivals, and was then making a poor living with a sewing-machine which she kept diligently in motion for that " universal provider " of Paris which passes under the romantic soubriquet of " La Belle Jardinière."

A visitor, in these last days, describes Verlaine as " sitting in an arm-chair near the open window ; his right leg swathed in bandages, resting on a stool." In his final illness, compact of causes rheumatic, alcoholic, and sexual, the poet did not want to go back to hospital, some surviving shred of the domestic instinct making him view death in a public asylum with something of horror ; and, being just then in funds, he bade Eugénie engage a maidservant, whom she took good care should be long past youth or any hint of its allure. Thus, well tended by hands which, though they belonged to a woman incapable of understanding him, whose attachment sprang from no higher motive than the gain it brought her, and cheered by the chirruping of the several canaries which tended to brighten the life of her quite cleanly and well-managed *intérieur,* Verlaine passed away, after calling out for Lepelletier and for Coppée before the coma finally stifled him, on the 8th January, 1896, at the age of fifty-two. He had been consoled by the last rites of his religion, but had lacked the kindly presence of any near friend or relation, by whom indeed the urgency of his condition was unsuspected. Eugénie, it is said, gave but a grudging welcome to his friends, whom she always distrusted as possible messengers from her rival Philomène to her poor charge, and she had sent them no warning of his fatal decline. She lost no time in turning every remnant of the poet's script and every relic, real or supposed, of his last days, into ready money. She survived him only a year.

XI

It is doubtful if any man has better understood Verlaine than François Coppée, who was so full of that pity that is akin to love ; and no fuller explanation of Verlaine's failings as a man and triumphs as an artist can be given than that implied by the touching words spoken by the poet of " *Les Humbles* " at the graveside of his dead friend—there re-echoing the words of all his best critics—" He remained a child always."

The world never lost its strangeness for him, and no burning of his hands in the flames could teach him to forbear from playing with fire, and the scar of old thorns was forgotten at the sight and the scent of new roses. The insatiable curiosity of an undeveloped intelligence was always his, the need for physical sensation which weakened him even while it soothed, and merely pricked an appetite that grew by what it fed on. The power of inhibition must have been wholly wanting, or at least subdued by a nervous system that clamoured and was appeased independently or even with the active pity or contempt of his spiritual choice. He was so far animal that all the five senses were to him monitors of strange powers often sinister and but seldom benign ; and so it came about that he fled for refuge to a theory that transcends the senses and their unceasing betrayal of our trust in them, a theory which, nevertheless, in Catholic countries, makes its human appeal through a ritual based on the emotions that upwell from sight and sound and the swinging of cloudy censers. Insane Verlaine undoubtedly was by the mere nature of his physical constitution, of which his mind was so pitiable a dependent. We must think of him then, not as a victim of drink, but as a victim to a nervous sensibility (of a nature quite imponderable to those who are without it), for which drink was the only palliative within his reach or knowledge. What might have been the saving and the healing influences in his life—those of his mother

and of his wife—were in hands too weak
and unstable to render them effective ;
and where the hands were strong and
masterful, as in the case of Rimbaud or the
pressmen who battened on his lamentable
decline, the influences were always to his
hurt. He followed impulse like an untamed
child that knows neither good nor evil, but
fulfils its need, and to whom that need's
suppression would appear merely as dis-
simulation for no obvious gain. " The soul
of an immortal child," says Charles Morice;[1]
" that is the soul of Verlaine, with all the
privileges and all the perils of so being :
with the sudden despair so easily distracted,
the vivid gaieties without a cause, the
excessive suspicions and the excessive
confidences, the whims so easily out-
wearied, the deaf and blind infatuations,
with, especially, the unceasing renewal of
impressions in the incorruptible integrity
of personal vision and sensation. Years'
influences, teachings, may pass over a
temperament such as this, may irritate it,
may fatigue it ; transform it, never—never

---

[1] Quoted by Mr. Arthur Symons in his "Symbolist
Movement."

so much as to alter that particular unity which consists in a dualism, in the division of forces between the longing after what is evil and the adoration of what is good ; or rather, in the antagonism of spirit and flesh. Other men ' arrange ' their lives, take sides, follow one direction ; Verlaine hesitates before a choice which seems to him monstrous, for with the integral *naïveté* of irrefutable human truth, he cannot resign himself, however enticing may be the passion, to the necessity of sacrificing one to the other, and from one to the other he oscillates without a moment's repose." It was that long oscillation on the tides of human impulse that left him socially derelict and without harbour gained. Nothing can better illustrate the helplessness and hopelessness of this oscillation than the account given by Mr. George Moore of his visit to Verlaine. " He had promised a friend of mine, a young enthusiast *décadent et symboliste*, a sonnet on Parsifal for his review. The sonnet had not arrived, and the review was going to press. Nothing for it but to start in search of Verlaine. . . . He said he was writing

the sonnet, and promised that we should
have it on the morrow. Then, in the gross-
est language, he told us of the abominations
he had included in the sonnet ; and seeing
that our visit would prove neither pleasant
nor profitable, we took our leave as soon as
we could. . . . After having given us an
abominable description in abominable language of the sonnet he was pondering, after
having sent my poor friend away in despair,
Verlaine sent him that most divinely
beautiful sonnet "—which we give here :—

Parsifal a vaincu les Filles, leur gentil
Babil et la luxure amusante—et sa pente
Vers la Chair de garçon vierge que cela tente
D'aimer les seins légers et ce gentil babil.

Il a vaincu la Femme belle, au cœur subtil,
Etalant ses bras frais et sa gorge excitante ;
Il a vaincu l'Enfer et rentre sous la tente
Avec un lourd trophée à son bras puéril.

Avec la lance qui perça le Flanc suprême !
Il a guéri le roi, le voici roi lui-même
Et prêtre du très saint Trésor essential.

En robe d'or il adore, gloire et symbole,
Le vase pur où resplendit le sang réel.
—Et, ô ces voix d'enfants chantant dans la coupole !

Here, in his art, he has indeed led his
captivity captive, and broken through his

enslaving chains, but in life he was never master of the means to that end. " The ideal world," says Mr. W. B. Yeats, of Verlaine's lamentably unbalanced behaviour among men, ". when it opens its fountains, dissolves by its mysterious excitement in this man sanity, which is but the art of understanding the mechanical world, and in this man morality, which is but the art of living there with comfort." Of Verlaine's life so viewed, it may indeed be said even more truthfully than of Pope's, that it was a " long disease," and though the martyrdom was self-inflicted and often paraded in a sordid guise, it was suffered for a principle—that of loyal surrender to the reality of emotional appeal and to its faithful presentment, without heed for any reasoned gospel of intellectual or social salvation, as being " wholly insidious and irrelevant."

His life, then, is but the trite old story of the emotions developed at the expense of domestic peace and civic order ; of art for art's sake made to condone the manner of its begetting, and the trend of its appeal ; of the hushed acquiescence in emotion as

a sacred thing, whatever the quality of the
impulse from which it ripens or the level
of the ideas on which it feeds. Nevertheless, his degeneration proceeded not from
the weakness of his mind, but in despite
of its fineness ; and no wallowing in the
mire with outworn harpies or gutter flot-
sam could quite quench his aspiration
towards the more excellent things. " To
be ashamed of nothing but to be ashamed
is his genius."[1] To a mind such as Verlaine's therefore, sinful to the brim, but
utterly without guile, confession was a
need that neither decency nor prudence
might restrain ; but let us not therefore
use his misfortunate babblings as a weapon
against him. Again, in the words of
Coppée, " Let us salute respectfully the
grave of a true poet, let us bow down before
the coffin of a child."

[1] George Moore.

XII

IT is curious to note how Verlaine, with
that somewhat haphazard and desultory
reading of English authors—from Shakespeare to Swinburne—from which he
gleaned much that helped him towards
that metrical freedom and fidelity to the
vagrom mood for which he is so especially
memorable, became in turn an influence
on those younger English contemporaries
whose names were associated with the
publication of the " Yellow Book," and
the more hectic afflorescence that whispered
to us of the roses and the raptures during
the nineties of last century. Verlaine's own
temper was entirely of Northern cast, his
feeling for the elusive and the forbidding
was quite Gothic, and but little compatible
with the clear sight and well-pondered
symmetry that are beloved by men who
draw their blood and their aspiration from
the meridional soil. To him the stupe-

faction of the reasoning mind by the on-rush of mere sensory perceptions was of the very stuff of poetry; and in his own work he mirrored both his ecstasy and its revulsion as in a troubled pool. The North was always magnetic to him; he repeatedly asserted it, always proud of his kinship with the *Nord;* and his own wanderings took him northward to Flanders, Holland, and our own shores.

The titles of many of his pieces—" Nevermore," " Birds in the Night," " Beams," " Streets," " Green "—prove what a power of suggestion lay for him in English words; he ardently admired and desired to translate Tennyson, and Mr. Francis Grierson reports him as saying, " Ah, what a difference there is between the word ' *mère* ' and the word ' mother ' ! The English word is soft, homely, and musical. I love the English language. There is the word ' heaven '; how much more beautiful it is than the word ' *ciel* ' ! English is made for sentiment and poetry." Though that opinion is not likely to be shared by many Frenchmen, we may yet take it, from our knowledge of Verlaine's leanings, as something more than the small change of conversational compliment; and there are but few of our poets since the time of its utterance who have not returned it by implication (however unwittingly) in their own work, by steering down the wide stream of influence that the speaker set flowing in more arid days. Such a lyric as Mrs. Meynell's " Chimes " is an instance of this conscious or unconscious derivation.

Verlaine's achievement in poetry and his influence on his own time may very properly be likened to the effects of impressionism, even of post-impressionism, in painting. He sought to convey an emotional impression for its own sake, without answering—at least consciously— to the need of interpreting intellectual or moral commentary. His whole life-work was, in principle, a refutation of at least three important *dicta* which have largely influenced criticism of English poetry (and thereby English poetry itself), since they were first uttered by three great exponents of the art of prosody.

" Invention is the polar-star of poetry,"

wrote Keats. Verlaine had none of it;
he was incapable of inventing. He ab-
sorbed through every pore of his spiritual
being whatever of material influence or
suggestion the five human senses can draw
in; and, for the stream of his song, he
tapped the cistern of experience.

"Great poetry is a criticism of life," said
Matthew Arnold. Verlaine, in the main,
gave forth his impressions without any
consideration of their relative importance
as sidelights on man's conduct and destiny;
certain things had happened, certain feelings had ravaged or consoled him, and
therefore, without the sophistication of
any conscious purpose, even, at times,
without coherence, he had quite literally
to *unburden* himself in song.

"Fundamental brain work" was Ros-
setti's demand. With Verlaine the brain
was nothing, while the nerve was all; and
to record the music of its vibrations—

> I who am as a nerve along which trail
> The else unfelt oppressions of the world—

whether the result in words were coherent
or not, was the only purpose relevant to
his art.

" Reflection in Verlaine is pure waste ; it is the speech of the soul and the speech of the eyes that we must listen to in his verse, never the speech of the reason."[1] Or to give again his own definition of his life's endeavour : " Sincerity, and the impression of the moment followed to the letter." Or again as Rodenbach has said of him : " He wrote as others pray." And in this constant responsiveness to the sway of emotional appetite, in his earthly wallowing and his heavenly aspiration and sweet penitence, he is road-fellow with the " *pauvre écolier* " François Villon, who trod yet wilder ways four hundred years before him, and left us, like Verlaine, ballads fit for brothels or for shrines.

Every art formula must go through the process of inception, development, and final running to seed, akin to the processes involved in the cultivation of physical types. Selection and adaptation through successive generations produce the perfect type, the patrician among men, and the cup-winner among animals. Then follows the self-stultification of inbreeding and

[1] Mr. Arthur Symons.

the perfecting of external form at the expense of inward vitality, the type becoming unfitted to any but the highly artificial and protective conditions which have produced it. Of no art is this truer than of poetry, where inspiration is seldom responsive to the incantations of a bygone ritual, Pegasus growing steadily tamer as his harness outwears. It is not that old forms are bad forms, or that the new ones in their turn do not become effete, but that, as soon as a type is finally achieved, the spirit that should inform it is apt to fly. What has become fixed can be learnt by rote and copied by those without the proper urgency of impulse that went to its first begetting. Drab sentiment and beggarly thought may assume the pontifical robes, while the true bearers of glad tidings, speeding hot-footed to the pulse of a new time, are conscious only of an impediment in such masquerading.

When Verlaine began to write, Hugo was enthroned as sovereign pontiff of French letters, and great as was his genius in verse, he was still of those who enlisted sympathy by rhetoric and by what Stevenson has called " a brutal assault on the feelings." It was none the less an assault on account of the pomp and circumstance of an approach that was deliberately calculated to cow the superstitious onlooker, and to flutter his heart by the waving banners and blaring trumpets of the outriders of Romance.

With Verlaine, that is, in the work that is truly *Verlainien* and not, as occasionally, a wistful dallying with the spent wave of classical or romantic impulse, there was no fixing of the stage, no bunting on a processional route, no reliance on stock sentiment, no " curtains." It was not his purpose to give us subjects of sensational or emotional appeal, but rather to show us, as his brothers of the brush were also doing, the results of sensation or emotion, set down as a musical effect, without betraying any predisposition of moral principle towards the thing expressed. His predispositions were those of taste and not of mind.

Even in his first volume, despite the overclouding Baudelairean influence, the true primitive stands revealed when we come

across a " *Croquis Parisien* " which we find,
in the words of Sainte-Beuve to the young
author, " *tout à fait piquant.*" The sim-
plicity and directness of its first stanza's
vision is clear and quaint as a child's
drawing on a slate :—

> La lune plaquait ses teintes de zinc
> > Par angles obtus
> Des bouts de fumée en forme de cinq
> Sortaient drus et noirs de hauts toits pointus.[1]

But the "*Soleils Couchants*" and the
" *Chanson d'Automne* " show already how
he can steep vision in emotion, and without any insistence on outline convey an
impression in words such as Sisley or Monet
were about to achieve in painting.

Again, we must remember that Verlaine
had no dramatic gift, that is, he was unable to evoke a variety of protagonists for
an equal variety of emotions ; himself was
his only mouthpiece, and he was played
upon by every wind of feeling that can
blow. We need not ask if Verlaine, turning momentarily aside from his ignomini-

---

[1] Let the reader remember that the usual French
clerk's 5 is other than ours, being more like an elongated
note of interrogation turned the wrong way round.

ous " *Chansons pour Elle* " to write a lofty exhortation to his son Georges, did so either with his tongue in his cheek or with a lively remorse for the sensual craving he had just left exploiting. The impulse was sincere in exact ratio as his art was successful whatever its theme, and it is irrelevant, as criticism of that art, to ask whether the impulse survived the moment of its inception and became a stable principle of mature thought driving to action. With Verlaine, thought apart from impulse could not dwell.

The method, of course, has its perils ; it means both artistically and socially living in a glass-house ; nor did Verlaine exempt himself from the disaster of thrown stones by his own forbearance in attacking others. The very principle of his art bade him wear his heart on his sleeve, and the daws were not lacking. Moreover, valuable as was, and is, the principle of a fair field and no favour to whatever subject the Muse sincerely affects, there will always be some gradation of fitness and of nobility, so long as men are an organized body with ideals of social welfare, and feelings to be hurt by their flouting. If mankind were only a rabble herded together for strength's sake all impulse might enjoy an equal sanction. But it does not, even with the hardiest of free-thinkers, whose theories recoil from action in the daily give-and-take of traffic with his own kindred. We do not imagine, therefore, that critics need be apologetic for looking somewhat askance at certain manifestations of Verlaine's wayward muse. With all respect to some warm-blooded apologists, we do not think that poetry born solely of the genitals will survive in the world's esteem so long as that poetry which, unconsciously subserving the social needs of our own and of all time, shows the disciplined spirit of man in conflict with a natural impulse deemed divine only when it is unhurtful. The discipline, of course, like the social needs, varies with the age and clime. But it is not passion alone which makes poetry, but passion at war with circumstances that corrupt, or conspiring with ideals that uplift it. And if, as has been claimed, all creative effort springs from the primary animal impulse, it is not less true that its beauty can only be expressed as the symbol of a reaching after something beyond its material fulfilment, and as the image of a life more perfect than the one now manifest ; and even though that symbol and that image be wholly illusory, there yet can be no beauty without them. We love Shakespeare's

> Look how a bird lies tangled in a net,
> So fasten'd in her arms Adonis lies,

but it is only slight and trivial poetry when compared to the sonnet beginning :

> Poor soul, the centre of my sinful earth,

the one exploiting the mere titillation of a passing appetite dependent on youth and the blood's heat, the other testing the spirit by that hard questioning that persists inwardly when the carnal need is spent, and by which, in the manner of our answering it, we prove our metal to be brittle or of enduring worth.

A specious and high-sounding phrase has been invented to excuse the perversities of imaginative genius by speaking of its achievement as a " conquest of new realms for the spirit." But the worth of such acquisitions depends on the nature of the territory, and if it be, morally, a malarial swamp conducive only to a human type found subversive in our normal world, it will always appear to the English mind that we shall do well to forgo the new kingdom and to withhold our homage from its discoverer.

Art is of all kinds, and success in each, however achieved, is its own justification ; so much of the " Art for Art's Sake " theory let us hasten to allow. But that " nice is nasty, nasty nice," and the creative artist the sole arbiter, must be hotly opposed so long as a social conscience survives. And by that same law which forbids (as Ruskin explained to us) a miser to sing of his lost gold though a maiden may sing of her lost lover, the meaner attachments of Verlaine's muse will be forgotten in his pæan to that Love, elusive though it be, that is " not Time's fool."

APPENDIX

THE quotations from Verlaine's work given in the preceding pages, inasmuch as they provide a moral commentary on their author's life (and they are given for that reason), are hardly typical of the vaguer Verlaine who wrought a tissue of imprecision into the fabric of French verse. The following renderings are an attempt, foredoomed perhaps to failure, to get in the translator's own way the effect achieved by their originals. General truth of impression has been sought even at the expense of literal fidelity ; and it is hoped that they may thus convey something of the mind of their original begetter to those whose knowledge of French may not be sufficiently intimate to yield it to them in his own tongue. To offer them to other readers would of course be an impertinence.

Page 10.
God spake and said, " Son, love me. Look and see
  My piercéd side, my shining heart that bled,
  And my maimed feet whereon the harlot shed
Her tears, and mine arms weighted painfully,

With burden of thy sins ! Behold the tree,
  Nails, gall, the sponge, and all that should avail
  To win thee from the world where lusts prevail
Unto my Flesh and Blood that calls for thee.

Have I not loved thee even unto death,
  O ! brother mine in God, dear child begot
  Of the same Holy Spirit ? My harsh lot
Have I not borne ? When direst sufferings rend
  I share thy sweat, I sob with thine own breath
Thy neighbour in the dark, O hapless friend !''

    Page 15.

Memory, what wilt thou with me ? Autumn gales
  Baffle the bird's flight through the moaning air ;
  The sun hurls wide his steady beams that stare
O'er the sere wood where thro' the north-wind wails.

We two alone, and both with dreams astray,
  With locks afloat in air and thoughts adrift,
  When suddenly to me her eyes uplift
And her voice asks, ''When wast thou happiest ? Say.''

As soft and song-like, as when angels chaunt,
  And my wan smile gives answer, else untold,
    And my weaned mouth along her white hand sips.
  No flowers have scent like that the first ones hold,
No sounds have such sweet stress as those that haunt
    The first-heard '' yes '' from the belovéd lips.

    Page 37.

All through the day down-poured the traitorous flame
  And lure of evil days. Now the sun's track
  Throbs with its glamour. Close thine eyes, turn back
From the most dire temptation—Fly the shame !

APPENDIX

Like hail the burning light hath downward sped,
   Despoiled the hill-side vintage, and left prone
   The cornfields of the valley, the blue zone
Even of redeeming heaven is ravishéd.

Then blench, and hie thee soberly to pray'r!
   If yesterdays devour the morrows' bliss?
      If madness, left behind, o'ertake thy way?
   Shalt thou not slay anew old memories?
For the last wild assault do thou prepare!
      And, lest the storm o'erwhelm thee, haste and pray.

Page 44.

         Long sob the violins
            Of autumn in the branches;
         The summer leafage thins;
            My heart grows sad to hear,
               So drearily, so wearily,
            The music drawing near.

         My breath goes in and out
            So quickly, my cheek blanches;
         The loud clock seems to shout
            " Beware! thine hour is near."
               So drearily, so wearily,
            My heart grows sad to hear.

         I mind me of lost youth
            How far away receded!
         How far they seem in sooth
            Those days that once were dear!
               So drearily, so wearily,
            I weep again to hear.

PAUL VERLAINE

Out in the miry ways
        I wander all unheeded ;
The rude wind round me plays
        And blows away my tear,
            So drearily, so wearily,
        A dead leaf of the year.

Page 59.

Then, let us part !   My word I'll not forswear
    Since I have thought so, it shall stand as true
    Whole and unbroke whatever men may do.
I will hold to it while this life I wear,

Though lofty spite nor grovelling scorn you spare.
    But like proud metal from the steaming brew
    Of smelted ore I will spring forth anew
Despite your tiresome friendship's noisome air. . . .

O ! for affection gentle and self-whole
That like a mossy nest may lodge the soul
    And fie ! then on the filthy " soul of Paris ! "

Long live French wit, Artois to Gascony.
Champaign and Argonne unto Burgundy,
    Long live the heart whereof kind memory tarries !

Page 62.

What beauty and what weakness may be told
    Of women whose oft-healing hands can crush,
    Their gaze wherein all fleshly power's at hush,
Save strength to whisper hot-blood churls " With-
    hold ! "

APPENDIX

Their voice that ever pain's spent cry controll'd
   With motherly solace, though with words forsworn,
   Soft chant of evensong, or call of morn,
Or sob that's smothered in a shawl's sleek fold!

Hard-hearted man! Vile life of sordid days!
   Far from love's soiled embrace and bartering
Somewhat shall hold even yet to loftier ways,
   Some throb of unspoiled heart unquestioning,
   Kindness and moral worth! For when death's wing
O'ertakes us at the last, then what else stays?

A SHORT BIBLIOGRAPHY[1] OF THE WORKS OF PAUL VERLAINE

POETRY

1866. *Poèmes Saturniens*. Paris : Lemerre.

1867. *Les Amies*. Scènes d'amour saphique. Sonnets. Par le licencié Pablo de Herlagnez. Bruxelles : Poulet–Malassis.

1869. *Fêtes Galantes*. Paris : Lemerre.

1870. *La bonne Chanson*. Paris : Lemerre.

1874. *Romances sans Paroles*. Sens. Typographie de Maurice Lhermitte.

1881. *Sagesse*. Paris : Société générale de librairie catholique.

1884. *Jadis et Naguère*. Paris : Vanier.

1888. *Amour*. Paris : Vanier.

1889. *Parallèlement*. Paris : Vanier.

1890. *Dédicaces*. Paris : Bibliothèque artistique et littéraire.

---

[1] The date of first publication alone is given here.

Femmes. Imprimé sous le manteau et ne se vend nulle part.

1891. *Bonheur.* Paris: Vanier.
Chansons pour Elle. Paris: Vanier.

1892. *Liturgies Intimes.* Paris: Bibliothèque du Saint-Graal.

1893. *Elégies.* Paris: Vanier.
Odes en son Honneur. Paris: Vanier.

1894. *Dans les Limbes.* Paris: Vanier.
Epigrammes. Paris: Bibliothèque artistique et littéraire.

PROSE

1884. *Les Poètes Maudits.* Paris: Vanier.

1886. *Louise Leclercq* (Suivie de Pierre Duchâtelet, Le Poteau, et Madame Aubin, un acte). Paris: Vanier.
Les Mémoires d'un Veuf. Paris: Vanier.

1891. *Mes Hôpitaux.* Paris: Vanier.

1893. *Mes Prisons.* Paris: Vanier.
Quinze Jours en Hollande. Lettres à un ami. La Haye: Blok, et Paris: Vanier.

1895. *Confessions.* Paris: Librairie du Fin de Siècle.

PAUL VERLAINE

1891.   *Les Uns et Les Autres.* Comédie en un
acte et en vers. Représentée pour la
première fois au Théâtre du Vaudeville par les soins du Théâtre d'Art,
le 21 Mai, 1891. Paris : Vanier.

POSTHUMOUS WORKS

1896.   *Chair.* Paris : Bibliothèque artistique
et littéraire.
Invectives. Paris : Vanier.

1897.   *Vive le Roy !* Drama en vers inédit
(fragment) *La Plume.* Avril.

1903.   *Œuvres Posthumes.* Paris : Vanier.

1904.   *Hombres.* Imprimé sous le manteau et
ne se vend nulle part.

1907.   *Voyage en France par un Français.*
Publié d'après le manuscrit inédit.
Paris : Messein.

PRINCIPAL REFERENCES

Œuvres complètes de Paul Verlaine (five vols.).
    Paris : Léon Vanier, 1899–1900.

Œuvres posthumes de Paul Verlaine (one vol.).
    Paris : Léon Vanier, 1903.

Paul Verlaine, sa Vie, son Œuvre, par Edmond
    Lepelletier. Paris : Mercure de France,
    1907.

Les Derniers Jours de Paul Verlaine, par F. A.
    Cazals et G. Le Rouge. Paris : Mercure
    de France, 1911.

Paul Verlaine, par Charles Morice. Paris :
    Léon Vanier, 1888.

La Vie de Jean Arthur Rimbaud, par Paterne
    Berrichon. Paris : Mercure de France,
    1897.

Jean Arthur Rimbaud, le Poète (1854–1873),
    par Paterne Berrichon. Paris : Mercure
    de France, 1912.

The Symbolist Movement in Literature [Paul
    Verlaine], by Arthur Symons. London :
    Constable and Co., 1908.

Impressions and Opinions, by George Moore. London : Werner Laurie (new edition), 1913.

Memoirs of My Dead Life, by George Moore. London : Heinemann, 1906.

French Profiles, by Edmund Gosse. London : Heinemann, 1905.

PERIODICALS

The Savoy, April, 1896.

The Fortnightly Review, July and September, 1894.

INDEX

INDEX

105

INDEX

PRINTED BY
WILLIAM BRENDON AND SON, LTD.
PLYMOUTH